Cantología I

PALABRA PURA POETS

ISBN: ISBN: 1940856000
ISBN-13: 978-1-940856-00-1
Library of Congress Control Number: 2013918670

DEDICATION

To all the poets, writers and storytellers that cannot remain silent.

Contents

ACKNOWLEDGMENTS

All proceeds of this publication, after costs, will benefit Palabra Pura, a program of the Guild Literary Complex.

Cantologia I

JUANITA GOERGEN

Casi poema de amor
…mostrarse alegre, triste, humilde, altivo creer
que un cielo en un infierno cabe
esto es amor, quien lo probó, lo sabe.
Lope de Vega, Soneto XII

En la orilla presentida bienquerido territorio,
margaritas deshojadas filtrándose en los abrazos
agua puesta en barrunto de septiembre detenidos:

cima en la cima del cielo
juntándose chispa y lumbre
desnudos y sin disfraces
en estrépito de enlaces
para inventar el amor

el amor
que es una flor en la orilla de los ojos
un aire tartamudeando en la lengua de un naufragio
un ave que anda al desvelo, espina con rosa hincada
sin sed, sin ala, sin vuelo

el amor
como una luna que baja por la escalera
como un manojo de versos
que temen ser un poema
porque el amor se acaba y se contiene
se finge distraído
la lengua casi al beso, pero no:
él y ella   -cáscaras de silencio-
ella y ella   -cáscaras de silencio-
él y él   -cáscaras de silencio-
mirándose de reojo, exhaustos
huyendo de lo exacto como huye el poema
que sabe que el augurio del amor, es más feliz,
que la querencia.

MARTHA CECILIA RIVERA

PENÉLOPE PROFANA

Incierta
la red se teje
indefinible
ecos de romanza
vaivenes

Refulgencias captura apenas
miradas de ola
  se quiebran en espuma
alientos de brisa breve
la sal
cuerpos

Rey, guerrero, poeta, sabio,
artesano, marinero
aguas quietas
de lejos, reflejo
traslúcidas de cerca
entelequias
serpientes
para una sola noche

Se pudren

Ni el que partió regrese
Ni playas interminables
ensortijadas
fábula de dioses
traigan nuevos cancerberos

Deshilvana
La libertad no miente

Martha Cecilia Rivera
Chicago, Julio 2013

LISA ALVARADO

The Botany of Hope
Think, at this blessed moment:
one thornless rose opens in the blue vase;
that tarnished bargain treasure that you, wanderer,
ferreted out of chaos.

You reading this — you know
nothing of how it came to flower there,
and I try to tell you that I wished it for you.
What knotted history twists its wild way
in your garden? That we can talk of easily, in
breathless laughter, between the war stories.

What flowers in secret
inside the walls of your chest?
Is it longing? Fear?
If I press my lips above your heart,
will my kiss set it free?

Listen to the wind, the way it sighs every night.
The gates of heaven never close,
that's our lesson, that's our imperfect miracle.

GROUNDWORK
How could I know
that deep in this frozen winter,
you would be an acquifer?

Acqua vitae
as warm as blood.

Agua Vida
feeding roots in the dreamless dark.
Sleeping so deep,
they had forgotten the memory
of trees.
.

EMANUEL XAVIER

HATS OFF TO THE BULL

I failed to see the signs along the way
confused by my needs
only to be told not to overthink,
overfeel, overwant, overdesire.

I didn't recognize the misery
I laughed with. The regret in your eyes
settled into your features, stories of
dead fathers, heartbreak, tears.

You did me no favors by holding back,
remaining distant as I longed for you,
sleeping alone with you right by my side,
contemplating your escape.

You once gave me a clock, aware
our time was running out. Your soul
belonged to the ghost haunting your life,
an empty house, full of could-have-beens.

Capable of change, I tried for us.
Not because you asked, because I was ready.
You have your freedom back. Now, lose yourself.
Just remember I was once a man

worth kissing. Goodbye. Hats off to the bull.
Believe in yourself and forget my sorrow.
Someday, I might smile at you again
and the red flags I will no longer ignore.

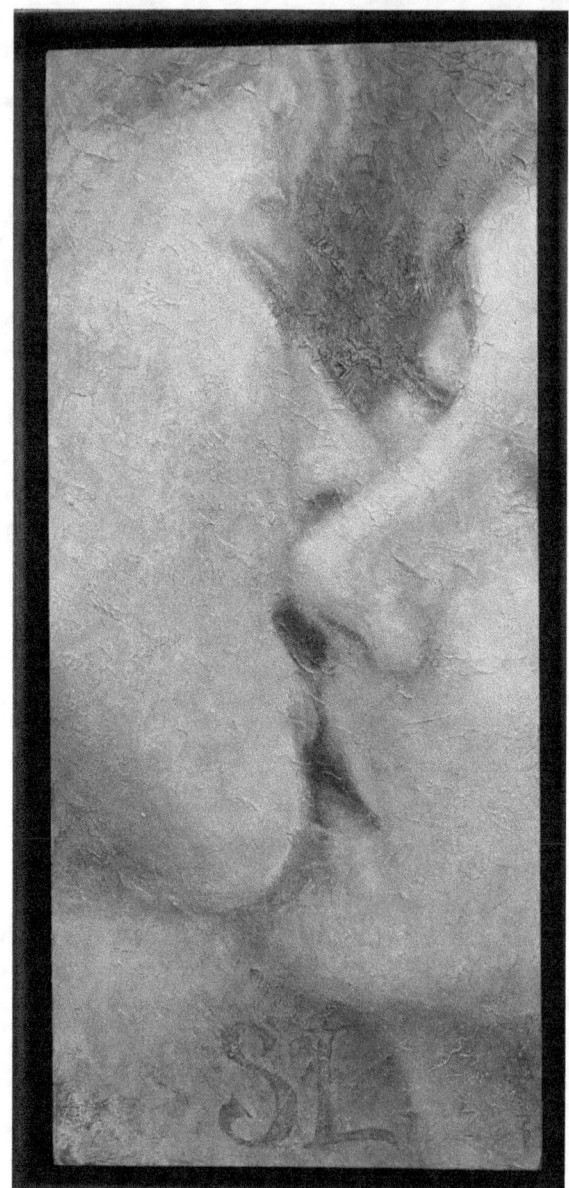

Elena Laura 1

XÁNATH CARAZA

Estremecimiento

Para Sacra líbido de Elena Laura

Se impregna de niebla la piel
Los párpados ceden al calor, luz del atardecer
El roce sutil se transforma en dorado aliento
Sístole, música interna, ritmos de la sangre

Penetra la humedad, explotan sílabas de la noche en el paladar
Pausada lectura de la poesía corporal
Suaves arabescos entre pulsaciones exhalo
La sangre se desliza en el cuerpo con intensidad

Ritmos internos de un instante, delicadeza
Inhalo fuerza, diástole azul, lentamente
La pasión de otra piel se intuye
Estremecimiento en el flamígero amanecer

Goosebumps

After Sacra líbido by Elena Laura

Their skin is bathed in mist
Their eyelids succumb to the heat, twilight
Their subtle touch motions into a gilded sigh
Palpating heart, inward music, rhythms of blood

Moisture seeps in, nighttime syllables on the palate burst
Intervals of incarnate poetry reading
Soft, intricate and intertwining artistry amid a pulse of exhaling
Blood runs down their bodies with fervor

Inward rhythms for an instant, gracefulness
I breathe vigor in, slow bluish expansion of the heart
The craze of another skin is felt
Goosebumps at opulent dawn

ELIZABETH MARINO

AMORE OR LESS

Love in the subbasement?
Cement, not hardwood floors?
No broad planks of oak?

Too much is plenty.
The love hungry never travel on their bellies.

Can windows be louvered
at the sidewalk?
No isenglass panels hang in mahogony frames.

We know we have no crystal stair.
Amore or less are we.

Can sheets and pillows be laid down
just right
so as never to be subject to eviction,
foreclosure or property tax abduction?

What we long for vs. what we have –
when I open my door, would you stand in its frame?

BEATRIZ BADIKIAN-GARTLER

NEW YEAR'S EVE
(with thanks to Toni Morrison
and Zora Neale Hurston)

He is my Ajax who brings me

a blood orange   red   red

dark red and sweet   I see

my first shooting star a few

minutes before the year ends

a new one begins   I make

a wish keep it secret   The sky

is black in Door County the road

empty   We ride silently while tall

pine trees whizz by festooned with

Christmas lights shining in the dark

beacons guiding us towards our new

life   too good to be true he says

He is my Tea Cake who teaches me

about music and painting takes me

to the seashore and the mountaintop

yes, it's too good to be true I nod

peeling my blood orange   Butterflies

escape filling every room in my heart

Incredulous at this new found love we
are like children swinging joyously
at a piñata that breaks open   Sweet candy
falling everywhere   We catch one piece two
blindfolded trusting laughter all around us

Beatriz Badikian-Gartler

PETER RAMOS

The Sound and the Fury

They came before language, a year after me. They came

back: seventeen-year cicadas. For weeks

they stared, red-eyed and vibrating, folded

under new leaves but driven in that heat

to mate and smash against glass.

They crawled up from under the ground,

mounting the trees as if they remembered, leaving

their delicate shells to the gnarled bark.

And when they'd let go, their song grinding higher

toward its impossible pitch, I'd come out of sleep as well, sweaty

and hard from dreamfucking a girl I was too scared to kiss.

I suffered valiantly, unrequited and polite

as the genteel poor, lonelier than a grown virgin. At night

I lay awake reading.   Those voices cut   the   day   like   a   saw.

SANDRA SANTIAGO

Woman Invisible

Woman the color of clay
moves in shadows and
works under the cover of night.
At home the babies soundly sleep.
Mami won't be missed.
She has made sure to leave bellies fed
And cheeks kissed

She is not soft.
No.
She is steel and backbone,
an equal to any.
She becomes an invisible gear
in the machination of industry.

Her limbs are a commodity.
Knees bowed to scrub floors
wiping up the drippings of
the day's residue from exhaustion
and sour ambition.
Legs and feet stand for 12 hours
at assembly line work
as once nimble fingers become
arthritic appendages
and language becomes a barrier,
a weapon for employee compliance.

Her limbs are a commodity,
calloused hands clean toilets,
season your food,
scour your pans,
scrub nasty soils from delicates.
Solid arms feed, hold and
tend to your babies
bringing comfort to your child
while leaving her own children's needs
in the hands of El Todo Poderoso.

Her limbs are a commodity.
Stooped back toils
to pick your tomatoes.
Her bladder leaks into
her pants and a supervisor
gropes her breasts.
Lungs inhale insecticide.
Tongue tastes the venom
as her blood pumps through
contaminated arteries .
Throat empty, void of voice
heart full of fear.
deportation and destruction
of family is not an option.

Her work is a baptism by fire
paying for her children's initiation
into the mainstream so that they
can say, "I too am America"

Sandra Santiago

Pandora lobo estepario press

DIANA PANDO

LOS DOMINGOS by Diana Pando

Los Domingos
I am
blue paint underneath
your fingernails.

Los Domingos is
when I want to find
the smooth
naked canvas of your
body lying next to me.

Los Domingos
all thoughts are like the cracked
walls of your art studio
chipping and
falling
apart
like me.

Los Domingos
Your snores
dance to early
morning cumbias
blasting out of
someone's car.

Los Domingos

Are filled with
blissful sighs
sleepy   yawns

Los Domingos
church bells ring
lovers twist
together like trensas

CANTOLOGIA I

Los Domingos
Stray dogs bark

Someone coughs

Pots and pans clank
up against each other

Los Domingos
draw up the curtains
letting the sun's rays

slowly

wander in

all the while

we

inhale

este domingo

Our Domingo.

CRISTINA CORREA

folding a sheet with my lover
there is no thrill purer than the rising
excitement of busy hands
on either side of a vast
and thin skin
combining folds to form a neat package
that smells of wet dough and settles
between the V our kneeling laps make
we find celebration in each
other's sloped eyes rejoiced
in the making of what has
always been

ROSEMARY ACEVEZ

"Todo Un Hombre Pa Toda Una Mujer"   November 4, 2009

Todo un hombre en que espejo lo puedo ver
Todo un Hombre que camino me guia a sus pies
Todo un hombre que libro leo pa entender

Toda una mujer aqui mi amor, aqui todo un hombre
Toda una mujer en la cama, la cocina, vestido y falda
Toda un mujer bolsa, esquina donde diario da vuelta

Hombre mujer mesa y sia inseparables
Mujer hombre fuego prendido y agua eterna
Hombre mujer profundo amor inconsolable

Pareja guantes de un solo mano mas bien el miton…
El baile #2 de los cosmos con maraca sagrada
Almas vibraciones destinados por las estrellas

Arboles majicos la yucca, acebuche, jobo y palo
Ojas exquisitos, gotitas de sangre
Monedas, palabras contra el viento

Santo dia logra cuando quere
Sudor del alma fuerza laborioso
Sueno dulce no hace falta pa realizar

Machi

MARTIN RUBIO

August's End

Once every blue moon
As they like to say
Guess that would be tonight
Mist surrounds the outside of her like
A white veil that I can't seem to pull back
There's this glow that somehow surrounds her
That she allows me to see in happenstance
This aura
Maybe there is hope around the horizon
I start to wonder if I could emit
That same kind of light
Reciprocating that warmth
Or if that was extinguished from me long ago
Here at August's end
Time stands still
And her face shows no sign
Of acknowledging my uncertainty
But I know that…she knows
Distant yet close
As we continue to stare at each other
We watch
Wait…
And wonder

Martin Rubio

ZULEMA MORET

"Otro Amor/ Amor Otro"

Amor el que se olvida de si mismo y apunta al otro que no es igual a si siendo parte de si como propone el tratado del cuerpo que Pablo dejara como testamento.

Amor incondicional como el de aceptar que no me amas de la manera en que deseo ser amada pero aún así te amo desde esta humanidad dolorosa.

Amor a ciegas como el que nos enseñaron en las telenovelas y radio y teleteatros, o desde la flecha impulsada por ese dios enceguecido que es Cupido. "Me quedé ciega de amor", te confesé.

Amor sin tocarse como el que algunos realizan a través de la esfera virtual sin olerse sin devorarse sin penetrarse, toda coraza, armadura.

Amor a solas como es todo amor excluido de si mismo apuntando al amanecer a la violeta extenuada del amanecer al rocío sobre la piel cayendo en la ladera de la soledad matutina.

Amor de ciudades abandonadas o despedidas desde algun avión que se diluye entre las nubes enrojecidas de olvido no de pasión.

Amor diluido en la Amistad, derramado por entre ríos que fluyen por los cráteres de las calles llenas de agujeros en los barrios perdidos de la memoria. Amor de animal a animal, cuando basta la Mirada para decodificar mensajes. Amor el de mis gatos a lo largo de mi vida no felina.

Amor inolvidable amor como dice la canción de la película en la que cuerpos traficados deben bailarla para exponerse al más salvaje de los intercambios al del no-amor, el del cuerpo convertido en mercancía.

Amor sin juicio ni celos ni música. Austero como las catacumbas en donde otro Amor se escondiera frente a la barbarie o al desconocimiento acogiendo a los primeros cristianos.

Digo Amor y aparecen ellos como partes del cuerpo de Cristo bailando, celebrando a cada momento la fundación de la vida, la construcción del Reino, plantando semillas de esperanza, en familia, en común unidad, mano a mano, sonrisa a sonrisa, lágrima a lágrima.

Digo Amor y desfila Juana de Arco muriendo en la hoguera con la sonrisa del sacrificio en la boca, digo Amor e imagino los estigmas de Caterina de Siena, centrados en esa mano que fue dedo apuntador para evitar la Guerra.

Digo Amor y huelo los excrementos, los restos humanos que oliera Madre Teresa por esas calles malditas de la India, invadidas de pobres enfermos abandonados a la mano del Amor, cuando el Amor se acercara como pura gracia del espíritu.

Digo Amor y Te veo entre choza, cabaña, hospital, salitrero, mina que se derrumba antes los ojos devoradores de la riqueza. Te veo ante los villeros mientras peregrinan sus vírgenes locales. Te veo ante la foto de Pepe Mujica, Te veo Amor del Otro iluminado, en la favela, en el rancherío, en la barriada, en el hospital, en la serena calma que anuncia la muerte o en la serena calma que cierran los ojos abiertos ante la violencia de la muerte.

Digo Amor y aparece Dorothy con sus 75 años en la cárcel en canto solidario con Cesar Chávez por las leyes agrarias y su protesta se ilumina en rayos como los que desprende el Corazón de Cristo, ella reclamando una habitación para otra persona que necesitara alojamiento. Dorothy resucita en cuerpo Amor en cada peregrino en busca de pan, de paz, de cobijo. Dorothy, ella la de la tan larga soledad.

Digo Amor y es cada fragmento de este gran cuerpo al que pertenecemos que se desvanece en partículas mudas frente a los tsunamis, los huracanes, los torbellinos, las inundaciones, los terremotos, desapareciendo entre objetos inútiles que se entrelazan ante el efecto desvastador de la tierra furiosa.

Digo Namaste y de tu espíritu a mi espíritu y viceversa un hilo invisible nos une hasta que la eternidad lo decida. Los nudos, los sueños que nos anudan por la noche, los reencuentros desde zonas que no conocemos, las pérdidas cuando los ojos se dan cuenta del error, de la imposibilidad.

Digo Amor y vuelo sobre la tierra, el planeta amado, miro las costas que alguna vez habité, los mares que me cobijaron jugando a amores futiles como los humanos, digo Amor volando por entre la vida, siendo resto, huella, poema en esta danza final.

YOLANDA NIEVES

Reality

Suddenly this dream you are having
matches everyone's dream, and the result is the world.
-William Stafford

Sometimes you have to wait
until someone sees you.

Then the words you speak
and the song you sing is alive;
you become beautiful.

It may take a long time.

JORGE GARCIA DE LA FE

Amor, ¿qué voy a hacer con tanta ausencia?

Amor, ¿qué voy a hacer con tanta ausencia?

Esa enorme antiflor, que transparente,

desampara mi boca, sonriente,

de tu lengua invasora. ¿Qué indecencia

revivir el gozoso desatino?

Desparramados trapos por el suelo

gimiendo quieren contemplar el duelo

de dos arcángeles ardiendo en vino

y rosas. ¿Qué mortales días volaron

por la turgente fruta de tus dedos?

¿Adónde iré esta noche con la sombra

de los rudos atletas que cruzaron

espadas en gimnásticos enredos?

¿Qué carcacola férvida nos nombra?

Jorge García de la Fe, Chicago, 28 de abril, 2013

DINORAH CORTES-VELEZ

A Love Note for Sister Lorde, Outsider

Por: Dinorah Cortés-Vélez

Soy el desequilibrio danzante de los astros.
Julia de Burgos, "Alba y desmadejada"

Mi muy amada hermana Lorde, forastera, me hablas en una lengua de fuego. Tu decir me irriga ríos de lava por la aorta. Agua, rumor, lengua. Caigo en la cuenta que, desde antes de conocerte, ya te aguardaba, con la espera acurrucada en la tensa calma del ojo huracanado.

Te escribo en la lengua de mi madre, la que ella me inculcó a amables dosis de ternura diluviada y de noches mañanas azul entrega, porque, aunque, astro-navegante de una nébula planetaria, ahora compartas el destino del sol, te urjo y me urges. Nos urgimos, con el vértigo de haber transitado juntas esa suave curvatura del agrado que es la sonrisa entre hermanas. Te escribo, Hermana Lorde, para decirte que de la arcana veta de tu letra, derivo la fuerza necesaria para afirmarme como una mujer identificada con otras mujeres, que te ama con el tierno furor de un relámpago anochecido contra la argenta superficie marina. ¡Tamaña dádiva de ti me has dado!

De ajonjolí y alegría, invocas, sempiterna, la antigua semilla. Tu voz, tierna, poderosa, deja abierta la herida de donde brota valiente tu poesía lumínica, gradual, musical y varia, como escala, mas, siempre, siempre, bella y gloriosamente negra, ¡como tú misma en ti, hermana!

Arregazada en tu decir me vivo en ti, arrebolada. Con el sano desequilibrio del aguacero, te canto. Un cuásar es tu senda, amada forastera del infinito. ¡Tamaña dádiva de ti, me has dado! Agua, rumor, lengua. Tu luz me intima que no es lujo ser poeta, que germina en la incomodidad la ventaja de la crisálida, y que en esa visibilidad alada que vulnera a la mariposa, radica su fuerza.

Acudo a la nomenclatura de tu particular conjuro y, para darle alas, danzo la danza obligatoria de mi mano con tus páginas. Mi muy amada hermana Lorde, forastera, te escribo esta carta de amor desde el corazón de la ventolera, despeinada y feliz. Agua, rumor, lengua.

TERESA VÁZQUEZ

Década

DJH

III.

Ya "shoeless" tiene nombre.

Es mas, lleva zapatos.

En el coche viaja atado seguro

Dirigido a casa de sus abuelos.

Su mirada apunta hacia atrás

No importa si vea cojín o los fascinantes lienzos celestiales

No importe la carretera que llevemos

Se le empaparán los sentidos.

Aquella es la posibilidad del nuevo ser.

Desde su percha, en lenguas duplicadas, se cersiora que andamos dotados :

"¿Zapatos/shoes? ¿Llaves/keys?

¿Carro mami? Daddy's truck?

¡OK, sí!"

él cachorra.

I.

En aquel anochecer

EL escote no se escondía

encaje rojo y negro

Sin ensayo saya y sayuela

Ardor que saludaba

Más allá de las rodillas.

El lino prefería cuello mandarino

Casi blanco. Sedosos pantalones de estreno

Acariciaban calzoncillos sueltos

Disimulando aumentos,

Bendito sea el acensor que al fín llegó.

Velas virginales

Exhalaban cera de abeja

Juntas al humo carnal

Aquel gotero marcando ritmo

Aguas misteriosas que fluían

Sobre dulces rubores

Paz por paso.

En aquel anochecer

Nos llamamos con nombres jamás pronunciados.

BEATRIZ RUIZ

Niñas y Lagartijos

If there are lizards near little girls
who can't sit the way they should,
the lizards will crawl up their legs
and feast on their wombs.

You don't understand;
I am that little girl and the lizards
have had their fill.

You are the best I can do
when I've carved my angular
apellido into my thigh
and all I can dream about are women.

You give me a daffodil
the day after I am obliterated.
I am bruised, so I accept.

You love me until
I resurrect myself.
I am teeth, blood, horns.
Soy una cabrona.
Y tu te revelas un lagartijo.

JENNIFER PATINO

Love in the Time of Guns
by Jennifer Patiño

You hear about the heads rolling, forty dead, highways clogged, highways watched, owned by sabe quien,   you hear about the camiones pulled to the side, the men unloaded and told, join us or die, you hear about the kidnappings, the ransoms sent too late, the narcofosas, the militares guarding funerals because you never know, your old roads, your old home are tributaries of hell, three cartels at least, three cartels, your tias get pizza one night and duck just in time, just in time for another fire fight, and now they lie, say they have no husbands, no children, keep them hidden, get down in the back, mi amor, get down in the back, and they've stopped nudging you, stopped asking ¿y tu cuando, mija-- que no te quieres casar? you hear about the partidos and the promises, this buey and that, and think if they were honest men, they'd be dead, you hear about Americans and their guns, Americans and their guns, their right to be scared of everything, shoot you on the border, shoot you in the theater, shoot your children, shoot you for looking, shoot you for looking wrong, shoot forty-six on the South Side, call it a Chicago weekend, shoot you before you come for their guns, but no, the American guns come for you, cross the border, make Mexico their new home, and the bodies climb, the thousands,   they climb by the thousands, and in the middle of all this you find some cover, find some love, someone who holds you and tells you sweet things, smiles teeth straight, a face that's never been punched, and he makes love like it's his religion, he wants you, his body, his everything gentle, you run your hands over his hips and let him kiss you, blink away the bullets, try not to imagine his corpse, try not to what if because you love and you've never been loved before, would give anything not to lose him, this, don't know how to pray, but your whole body aches in all directions, "please," for him "please," but nena, the only thing you know is that you never know, so you kiss him harder now

RITA MARTINEZ-PUCIO

JANE EYRE DREAMS OF RESCUING HELEN BURNS

She hacked bloody mucous, made two fists,
then pummeled her chest trying to breathe.

I woke to the sight of her lifeless form,
one hand splayed against the bedrail,

the other still gripping an inhaler. I've traced
the inscription on her tombstone with my forefinger.

But she can't be dead. I think of her when AMBER Alerts
flash, suspect Brocklehurst and Scatcherd faked her death,

then auctioned her to a child prostitution ring in Guatemala
or perhaps as a mail-order bride in Thailand

where she's bewildered by the language and landscape,
by swarms of balding men, each old enough to be her father.

In my daydreams, she kneels and prays God will appoint me
the agent of her deliverance. After rescuing Helen we return

to Northumberland where she wanders across familiar
moorland, observes curlicues soaring overhead,

bills curled downward in greeting. Helen's eventually adopted
by wealthy New Zealanders, doting parents who say her beauty

surpasses Helen of Troy's as they tuck her in bed.
I imagine she has many pets. Her favorite a pair of sheep

named Francis and Clare. Helen takes them to show and tell,
parades them at local fairs, displays award ribbons and medals

beside the gold-enameled teapot in her mom's china cabinet.
She dresses as Little Bo-Peep on Halloween and takes

Francis and Clare trick-or-treating, makes rounds at nativity plays,
the placid sheep always reposing beside baby Jesus' manger.

As an adult, Helen transitions from beloved Sunday school teacher
to well-known televangelist, millions tuning in to hear the Word

as they sip morning coffee. The image of Helen's kind face
and relaxed demeanor while reading scripture remains with them,

changes their lives in subtle ways. Audience members refrain
from biting their nails, cutting in traffic or at checkout,

from spanking their children for minor offenses. A stanch viewer,
St. John admires Helen's dynamic preaching and missionary work.

He shreds Rosamond's picture. After a brief introduction and whirlwind
romance, St. John and Helen exchange vows and head to India

where camera crews film their experiences as part of a new Christian
reality show. Always a brainiac, Helen's aptitude for languages

enables her to pick up Hindustani faster than I ever could.
A byproduct of Scatcherd's punishments, she's developed a high

threshold for tolerating discomfort and never complains of sweltering
heat.
Her indomitable spirit always inspires St. John's fervent admiration.

A devoted husband, he thanks his Maker for Helen's piety and
patience—
for the beautiful blaze of hair he happily unpins and brushes after evening
prayer.

XENIA RUIZ

Lover
who are thee to me?
let me see
my cho-co-la-te lover
as you creep into my den
of deseos
in the dead of night
like some vampiro
and sink thine teeth
into my paraiso

who are thee to me?
let me count thy dedos
as they pry open my mane
and massage my skin
til it aches for your scratch
let me add thy besos
as they multiply
over my forbidden temple
until you fall upon your knees
and worship and please me

who are thee to me?
my cho-co-la-te lover
I love thee
like bigots love to hate
and bakers love to bake
thou art just like
a pantera stalking his game
a brave counting coup

who are thee to me?
you ask
my cho-co-la-te lover
as you slither out the door
of my queendom
until the next oportunidad
presents itself

you are
what you are
my lover

my cho-co-la-te lover
my negro, creole, mulato
night-time, sometime lover
so like the others
who came before
and will come after
happily
ever
after

EDUARDO AROCHO

Mundillera

Busco un cuento en el mundillo
De Chepa
Busco un cuento en el mundillo
De Viña
Busco un cuento en el mundillo
De Moca

Fui para el Chimbí
Donde pobres nacieron ellas
De tez Monserrate negra

Y fui para Moca Garden
Donde vi la autora morena
De ojos azules, meticulosa
Escritora de patrones innumerables

Oigo las campanas de la iglesia
Oigo el ritmo de los bolillos,
Que bailan con dedos jóvenes y viejos,
Escondiendo bochinches feos
Y tejiendo margaritas maravillosas

Que mucho ha cambiao Moca
Ha cambiao con Puerto Rico
Ya no existe el viejo camposanto
Pero todavia se llama Moca
Donde todavía se hace mundillo

Busco un cuento en el mundillo
De Chepa
Busco un cuento en el mundillo
De Viña
Busco un cuento en el mundillo
De Moca

No viven en castillos

Pero son reinas de Moca
Mundilleras, prefieren vestir
Con batas de casa
Pero bordan bellos trajes de boda

Nunca se ponen viejas
Esas mundilleras
Porque siempre están tejiendo
Coronas pa' bebes.

Nunca se ponen viejas
Esas mundilleras
Porque siempre estan tejiendo
Botines pa' bebe

Aquí Chino tocaba trompeta
Donde siempre hilos y puntos
bordados en la historia,
Por eso nunca descansan los alfileres
Por tanto tiempo en cojines

Sí, yo encontré a Chepa
En el mundillo

Y encontré a Viña
Haciendo mundillo

Y encontré a Moca
Viviendo con el mundillo

Orgulloso está Puerto Rico
De su mundillo

SILVIA GOLDMAN

El nombre no es mío es de Silvia. En el fondo de su pie se agita el afuera y la familia que ella es dentro del aire. Oloroso piedra con piedra en la claridad del nosotros es pozo que toca su pérdida. Es niña que pasa en rincón que no sale. Es mujer que gana por herida. Es aire amparando su punta blandiendo lo sentido lo que no gravita. Es la cena es los hechos el dedo que pone su mañana la espalda en que ella corre. Es tumbar lo que se dan. Juntar los cuerpos con lo grave. Reposar.

El odio y el amor se ensanchan en un vagón de carga
dos madres hacinadas pariéndose los bordes
contándose los pliegues las arrugas
abajo las lenguas se endurecen
salen a pescar
el llanto de sus hijos.

JOHANNY VÁZQUEZ PAZ

DESTINO DE UN NOSOTROS

Sé que algún día nos volveremos a encontrar. Tú y yo estaremos frente a frente, sin planearlo ni ponernos de acuerdo. Escucharás el taconeo de mis pasos y el recuerdo de callejones alterará tu rumbo. Yo me arrepentiré de la selección de ropa, y tú de llegar acompañado. Veré en tus ojos el resplandor de mis palabras. Leeré en tus ojeras las huellas de un poema amanecido. Escucharé la melodía que compones al leerme con las letras que escribí pensando en ti. Tú que me descifras en el silencio de esta intimidad compartida en la distancia. Tú que me deseas furtivo en tu anonimato. Te reconoceré por el olor a versos que exhalas con cada parpadeo. Escucharé mi voz como un coro de cánticos sagrados. Te ofreceré mi mano repleta de verbos que esperan realizarse en tus ojos. Me sentiré útil frente a ti, y tú te sentirás mi cómplice. Nos vamos a encontrar de nuevo, te lo aseguro. Ya los versos del destino están impresos.

MARY HAWLEY

$1 + 1 = 11$

August 11, 2013

It isn't logical except in a unary number system, in which $1 + 1 = 11$ and
$1 + 1 + 1 = 111$ and so on but 11 means 2. We two are eleven years into
this

binary system of marriage not too often ornery or unaware, even as we
explode
with everything else into airless space with its cold and paradoxical
winds

spinning in the dustcloud of the star that could be named Matrimony or
Joyride
with Two Steering Wheels. We look forward and back and there are
losses

both ways. We are alone together like the unary candles on a birthday
cake, each
saluting its own starry year. Starlight streams toward us from eons
before a twinkle

in your father's eye was the spark of you as your young and beautiful
mother went
into his arms. What spark moved us from caution to swimming in the
same deep lake

under those oblivious stars? Our natures are in sympathy or symphony.
And yet
there are spaces between us that armchairs or elephants could fall
through before

a solar wind whisks them away. Remember what the proton said to the
electron:
Can't you be more positive? What I have is you—plus a few billion
moments

like the sun in our faces after days of rain. And you have me: gifts we
cannot fully
understand except over a lifetime, which coincidentally is how long we

have. (Or

more? If it goes my way I will find you under our new stars, wherever they are,
and won't say I told you so—of course, if it goes your way, neither will you.)

MIGUEL LOPEZ LEMUS

Su mejilla
piedra de río
incendiada de sol;
cristal incauto
y correr de gaviotas,
su mirar
una noche, en San Cristóbal
me detuve al final de una larga calle
apenas iluminada por algunos faroles débiles
y me quedé silencioso
sin poder decir nada
con la calle desierta
impregnándome de color,
dejándome marcado para siempre,
a tu lado me quedo silencioso
sin poder decir nada,
con el alma desierta
impregnándome de color
dejándome marcado para siempre,
a tu lado el sol incendia
el cristal incauto de gaviotas,
valles corridos,
recorriendo piedras y ríos
al final de una larga calle
incendiada de ti.

BIOGRAPHS

Beatriz Badikian-Gartler

Beatriz Badikian-Gartler was born and reared in Buenos Aires, Argentina, and has lived in the Chicago area for over forty years. Badikian-Gartler holds a Ph.D. in English from the University of Illinois at Chicago and teaches at various institutions of higher learning, including Northwestern University, Loyola University, Roosevelt University, and others. Her essays, poems, and stories have been published in numerous journals, anthologies, and newspapers in the United States and abroad. She is a popular performer in the Chicago area and lectures often on women's issues, art, and literature. In 2000 Badikian was selected as one of the One-Hundred Women Who Make a Difference in Chicago by Today's Woman magazine. She is an Illinois Humanities Council Road Scholar and a frequent Newberry Library instructor. Her second full length collection, Mapmaker Revisited: New and Selected Poems, was published in 1999 from Gladsome Books in Chicago. Her first novel Old Gloves – A 20th Century Saga was published in 2005 by Fractal Edge Press in Chicago. For more information take a look at her website: www.bbgartler.com and visit her blog: gartlerwritingstudio.blogspot.com.

Beatriz Ruiz

Beatriz J Ruiz was born and raised in Chicago and Guanajuato. She is a writer by vocation, not profession. She is not a gold coin. She has always tried to find home but instead has chosen to carry it on her back. She is an osicona, a chingona, casada pero no embarazada. She is the boxer's swan song.

Cristina Correa

Cristina Correa attended the Ragdale Foundation as a 2013 Midwestern Voices and Visions awardee and is a VONA alum. Her fiction and poetry have appeared in Rebelde: A Proyecto Latina Anthology, As/Us Journal, Kalyani Magazine, and Ariel XXX. She has been a featured reader at various local series including Revolving Door and Palabra Pura. She holds a BA from Columbia College's Fiction Writing Department and is an MA candidate in Latin American and Latino Studies at the University of Illinois at Chicago. A born-and-raised Chicagoan, Correa currently lives in Humboldt Park.

Diana Pando

Diana Pando is a writer from Chicago and a founder of the Proyecto Latina Reading Series. She also writes for the Proyecto Latina online site and has interviewed countless of Latinas making an impact in the arts and media. In 2012, her poem Coatlique Rising was selected to be part of the Rites of Passage anthology published by Mujeres de Maiz in California and was a finalist for the Gwendolyn Brooks Poetry Competition. In 2010 her ten-minute play Thirst was presented at Teatro Luna's 10X10 play festival. Her poem Stanislao In Sepia was also featured in the Ariel XXVIII journal. Currently she is part of the Con Tinta literary advisory board. Follow her on Twitter @dianapando

Dinorah Cortes-Velez

Dinorah Cortés-Vélez is from Isabela, Puerto Rico. She has resided in Wisconsin since 1997. In 2011, she published her first novel, El arca de la memoria: una biomitografía, (The Chest of Memory: A Biomythography) with Editorial Isla Negra (San Juan, Puerto Rico). Her second book of fiction, Cuarentena y otras pejigueras menstruales (Quarantine and Other Menstrual Trifles), has also been published recently with Editorial Isla Negra. She is an Associate Professor of Latin American literature at Marquette University, Milwaukee, WI, USA. She earned her doctoral degree at the University of Wisconsin-Madison with a dissertation on the ethical and political uses of humor in Sor Juana Inés de la Cruz. Her research interests include colonial and contemporary Latin American literature. She is a regular contributor of the Puerto Rican newspaper El Post Antillano (http://www.elpostantillano.com/).

Elizabeth Marino

Elizabeth Marino is a Puerto Rican poet and educator, based in Chicago. Her chapbook, Debris: Poems and Memoir, went into a second printing (Puddin'head Press 2011). She was awarded Hispanic Serving Institution funding from NEIU for her Latina/o Community Creative Non-Fiction Workshop and received a 2012 CAAP grant and conference scholarship to attend the initial Las Dos Brujas Writers' Workshops, where she studied with Juan Philipe Herrera, poet laureate of California. She was a Ragdale resident and holds an MA from UIC's Writers' Program in addition to having studied literature at Oxford University on academic scholarship. Elizabeth's poetry has appeared in print journals, anthologies and live performance. Currently, she is working on a second chapbook, Ceremonies,(forthcoming from Dancing Girl Press), and conducts a creative writing workshop for GLBTT seniors at The Center on Halsted. Most recently, her work was given a critical review in Femficatio (London), and also appeared in the national Latino blog of culture and literature "La Bloga", along with the FB page "Poets Responding to SB 1070."

They say "live and learn." Poetry helps me do both.

Emanuel Xavier

An Equality Forum LGBT History Month Icon, Emanuel Xavier is a poet and author of Ecuadorian/Puerto Rican heritage. As a former homeless gay teen.and survivor of child abuse, he has staged many benefits for queer youth and is a longtime LGBT rights activist. He is author of the poetry collections Nefarious, If Jesus Were Gay & other poems, Americano: Growing Up Gay and Latino in the USA, Pier Queen and the novel Christ Like. He is also editor of Mariposas: A Modern Anthology of Queer Latino Poetry and Me No Habla With Acento: Contemporary Latino Poetry. He appeared on Russell Simmons presents Def Poetry on HBO and has performed in cities throughout the United States, Buenos Aires, Ghent, London and Paris. His poems have been translated into Spanish, French and Romanian, staged as a choreographed dance presentation and remixed into House dance tracks. He released an audio spoken word/music collaboration album, Legendary, available for digital download.

Jennifer Patino

Artist Statement

It is not often that I write love poetry. Poems about politics, the politics of being a Latina in Chicago, in this country, of missing home, the politics of sex, even—those are familiar territory. But love poetry, is something that takes more courage than I'm capable of sometimes. Sweet words don't come easily. I love like a ferocious thing, a woman raised by wolves. It's easier to say "I will break the world in half for you," than it is to say "Please world, don't break my heart." Dear reader, I love and thus am at your mercy. My love moves through the world, frail as any human and defenseless. Your love does too. Let's be kind.

Whether in the heart of Chicago or the heart of Guanajuato, Jennifer Patiño has always lived in the Midwest. She has written and edited for Latina Voices and Gozamos, has published in the South Loop Review and recently joined the Executive Board of the online arts publication Sixty Inches From Center. She is a poet, essayist, columnist and feminist who was most likely burned as a witch in another life.

Johanny Vázquez Paz

Johanny Vázquez Paz nació en San Juan, Puerto Rico. Ha publicado los libros Querido voyeur (Ediciones Torremozas, Spain, 2012) y Poemas callejeros (Mayapple Press, Michigan, 2007) el cual ganó premio en el International Latino Book Awards (California, 2008). En el año 2012, recibió el primer premio en poesía en el Concurso de Cuento y Poesía

Consenso de la Universidad Northeastern Illinois. Además, recibió el segundo premio en el mismo certamen por su cuento "La muda". Coeditó la antología Between the Heart and the Land / Entre el corazón y la tierra: Latina Poets in the Midwest (MARCH/Abrazo Press, 2001). Su trabajo ha sido incluido en las antologías City of Big Shoulders, Ejército de rosas, En la 18 a la 1, The City Visible: Chicago Poetry for the New Century y Poetas sin tregua-Compilación de poetas puertorriqueñas de la generación del 80, entre otras. Actualmente es profesora de español en Harold Washington College en Chicago, IL.

Johanny Vázquez Paz was born in San Juan, Puerto Rico. Her book, Querido voyeur, was published by Ediciones Torremozas (Madrid, Spain, 2012). Her previous book Streetwise Poems /Poemas callejeros (Mayapple Press, 2007) won an award in the 2008 International Latino Book Awards (California). On 2012 her collection, "Sagrada familia" (Sacred Family), won first prize in the poetry category at the Consenso Short Story and Poetry Contest of Northeastern Illinois University. She also won in the same contest the second prize for her story "La muda" (The Mute). She co-edited the anthology Between the Heart and the Land / Entre el corazón y la tierra: Latina Poets in the Midwest published by MARCH/Abrazo Press in 2001. Her work has been included in the anthologies City of Big Shoulders, Ejército de rosas, En la 18 a la 1, The City Visible: Chicago Poetry for the New Century, and Poetas sin tregua of Puerto Rican poets from the 80's generation, among others. She currently teaches Spanish at Harold Washington College in Chicago, IL. The author invites everyone to her blog TINTA DERRAMADA at: http://johannyvazquezpaz.blogspot.com/

Juanita Goergen
Juana Iris Goergen (Puerto Rico). Published poet. Professor of Spanish, Latin American and U.S. Latino Literature at DePaul University, Chicago. As a poet she has published La sal de las brujas (finalist of Letras de Oro and published by Betania 1997) and La piel a medias (2001), Las Ilusas/Dreamers (Vocesueltas, 2008) as well as poems published in anthologies: Astillas de luz/Shards of Light (1998), Nosotros los otros (1996) Between the Heart and the Land/Entre el corazón y la tierra (2001), Generación (2001) among others. She is the editor of the anthologies: Susurros para disipar las sombras (2011) and Rapsodia de los sentidos (2012) (Erato ediciones, Poesía en abril International Poetry Festival v & VI). She developed and co-organizes in Chicago, Poesía en abril: International Poetry Festival in Spanish, now in its 7th year. She has two unpublished poetry collections: La celda de Lilith and ContraOda al sueño americano.
Poeta. Professora de Literatura Latinoamericana en la Universidad San

Vicente DePaul en Chicago. Ha publicado La sal de las brujas (finalista del premio Letras de Oro, Betania 1997) y La piel a medias (2001), Las Ilusas/Dreamers (Desarraigos, Vocesueltas, 2008). Su poesía aparece en las antologías: Astillas de luz/Shards of Light (1998), Nosotros los otros (1996) Between the Heart and the Land/Entre el corazón y la tierra (2001), y Generación (2001) entre otras. Ha editado las antologías: Susurros para disipar las sombras (2012) y Rapsodia de los sentidos (2013), ambas (Erato ediciones: Festival de poesía/Poesía en Abril V y VI). Es iniciadora y co-organizadora del Festival Internacional de Poesía en Español: Poesía en Abril, en la ciudad de Chicago, actualmente en su séptimo año. Tiene inéditos dos poemarios: La celda de Lilith y Contra-Oda al sueño americano.

Jorge García de la Fe

Jorge Luis Garcia de la Fe: Born in Cardenas, Cuba, Sept. 25, 1954. Poet, writer, and former editor of the journal Contratiempo. Live in Chicago since 2007. Received his BA in Literature from the University of Havana (1975-1981) and MA in Latin American Literatures and Cultures from Northeastern Illinois University (2011-2012) Between 1981-1996, Garcia de la Fe was professor of Literature at Juan Marinello, a Higher Education Institute in Matanzas, Cuba. He also worked as Art Methods Teacher at the Guanajayabo Cultural Center in Maximo Gomez (1996-2002), as well as professor of Spanish Stylistics at Camilo Cienfuegos University in Matanzas (2002-2007). Since 2007 lives in Chicago where he has taught at Cervantes Institute, Centro Romero, Enlace-Chicago and St. Augustine College. His poems have been published in Revista Matanzas (Cuba); Ventana Abierta (California); El Canto del Ahuehuete (León, Guanajuato); Contratiempo (Chicago); Dialogo (DePaul University, Chicago). His poetry collection Chicago es mi batey/Chicago is my Community has been published by Vocesueltas 2010, in the Collection En la 18 a la 1/ In the 18th. At 1. His poems are also part of the anthologies Susurros, para disipar las sombras (Erato, 2012) and Rapsodia de los sentidos (Erato, 2013). At present he works as a professor of Spanish at Harold Washington College.

Jorge Luis García de la Fe: Nació en Cárdenas, Cuba el 25 de septiembre de 1954. Estudió una Licenciatura en Lengua y Literaturas Hispánicas en la Universidad de la Habana entre 1975 y 1981 y un Master en Literaturas y Culturas Latinoamericanas en Northeastern Illinois University entre 2011 y 2012. Fue profesor de Literaturas Hispánicas en el Instituto Superior pedagógico "Juan Marinello" de Matanzas entre 1981 y 1996. Trabajó como Metodólogo de Arte en la Casa de Cultura "Guanajayabo" de Máximo Gómez entre 1996 y 2002, así como profesor de Redacción y Estilo en la Universidad "Camilo Cienfuegos" de Matanzas entre 2002 y 2007. Emigró a Estados Unidos en 2007. Reside en Chicago, donde se ha desempeñado como profesor de Español y GED en el Instituto Cervantes, Centro Romero, Enlace-Chicago y Saint Augustine College. Es poeta, ensayista y ex-editor de la revista Contratiempo. Ha publicado sus poemas y ensayos en: Revista Matanzas (Cuba), Ventana Abierta (Santa Barbara,California), El Canto del Ahuehuete (León, Guanajuato), Contratiempo (Chicago) y Diálogo (DePaul University). Su poemario Chicago es mi batey forma parte de la antología En la 18 a la 1, publicado por ediciones Vocesueltas en septiembre de 2010. También forma parte de las antologías poéticas Susurros, para disipar las sombras (Erato, 2012) y Rapsodia de los sentidos (Erato, 2013). Actualmente labora como profesor de Español en Harold Washington College.

Lisa Alvarado

Lisa Alvarado is a poet, performer, and installation artist and is the author of two award-winning chapbooks, Reclamo and The Housekeeper's Diary; the latter also a one-woman performance which toured nationally. Lisa is also the co-author of the acclaimed young adult novel, Sister Chicas, written with Ann Hagman Cardinal and Jane Alberdeston Coralin. She is the recipient of grants from the Department of Cultural Affairs, The NEA, and the Ragdale Foundation, and is also a journalist, contributing reviews and interviews to La Bloga, and Blogcritics.org

Martha Cecilia Rivera

CREDO POETICO

Solo cuando un poema se ha bebido todo mi aliento, cuando ya no hay nada más que yo pueda darle, solo entonces está listo para perseguir su destino de pluma leve, mínima, que vuela para buscar al Otro en esa inmensidad compartida e irrepetible llamada el alma humana.

Martin Rubio Jr.

Martin Rubio Jr was born and raised locally in Pilsen. He began writing poetry and prose early on, and his first works appeared in the underground magazine called Zacapuntas. Early local influences were Carlos Cortez and Carlos Cumpian. As the work progressed, he recited at places he would frequent as a spectator. Places like Cafe Jumping Bean, Lit X, and most recently Weeds. He also had the opportunity of featuring in Palabra Pura's "Lives Between Love and Darkness" in which was curated by Gregorio Gómez in the spring of 2012.

Mary Hawley

Mary Hawley is the author of Double Tongues, a poetry collection, and co-translator of the bilingual poetry anthology Astillas de luz/Shards of

Light. She works as a freelance writer, editor, and translator, and is currently the coordinator of the Guild Complex's Palabra Pura bilingual reading series. Her poems have appeared in journals and anthologies such as Mudlark, Notre Dame Review, contratiempo, and Power Lines: A Decade of Poetry from Chicago's Guild Complex.

Miguel Lopez Lemus
Multi-media artista

Peter Ramos
Peter Ramos's poems have appeared in Colorado Review, Puerto del Sol, Painted Bride Quarterly, Verse, Fugue, Indiana Review, Mississippi Review (online), and other journals. He is the author of one book of poetry, Please Do Not Feed the Ghost (BlazeVox Books, 2008). His criticism has appeared in College Literature, The Faulkner Journal, The CEA Critic, Mandorla, Verse, Pleiades and Poetry Daily. An associate professor of English at Buffalo State College, Peter teaches courses in nineteenth- and twentieth-century American literature.

Rita Martinez-Puccio
Rita Maria Martinez's work has been featured in the eighth edition of Stephen Minot's Three Genres: The Writing of Fiction/Literary Nonfiction, Poetry and Drama (Prentice Hall) and in Burnt Sugar, Caña Quemada: Contemporary Cuban Poetry in English and Spanish (Simon & Schuster). Martinez's first chapbook, Jane-in-the-Box, takes a character from classic English literature—Jane Eyre—and revamps her with tattoos, fishnets, and modern feminism (March Street Press). Her poem "St. John Rivers Pops the Question on Jane Eyre" was nominated for a Pushcart Prize. Martinez is an Academic Services Writing Consultant for Nova Southeastern University. She lives in Miami, Florida, with husband Todd Puccio.

Rosemary Aceves
All my poetry is written as Machi
I write poems both in English and Spanish
I attended Columbia College, where I studied liberal arts
My interest in writing started around 8 or 9 years of age
I've read and continue to read my poetry at:
Weeds, Green Mill, Palabra Pura and Butterfly Project -
I recently participated in the outdoor Broken Windows event
coordinated by The Guild Complex and which appeared on
CAN TV, and posted on youtube
Luz y Paz, Machi

Sandra Santiago
Sandra Santiago, "La Pixie" is a branch from two limbs of differing trees, intertwined haphazardly. Youngest daughter of Tomas Santiago and Rosa Feliciano. She is a Chicago based educator, activist, published artist/illustrator, artisan, performance poet and actress. She has her B.A in education from Roosevelt University Chicago, Illinois. She has been an early childhood educator for the Chicago Public Schools since 1997.

She has published her poetry in several anthologies including The Poetically Unspoken Anthology (2010), Shades of Faith; Minority Voices in Paganism Anthology and The Journal of Ordinary Thought (Fall 2009 and Winter 2009), and the on-line journal, Everyday Ordinary Things and Dicen Quien Dicen. Sandra will have poems published in The Proyecto Latina Anthology and the online zine Brown Queen summer 2013

Sandra is part of the original cast of the Vida Bella Ensemble (Brown Girls' Chronicles: Puerto Rican Women and Resistance, Bless Me Madrina). She was a write/performer for The Guild Complex's Tour Guides (2010). She was also part of a rotating ensemble with Beastwomen at Chicago's Greenhouse Theater (2010-2012). She continue to performs and has featured at various venues throughout Chicago and New York Momma's Hip Hop Kitchen.

Sandra has performed at various universities including, University of Illinois at Chicago, University of Illinois in Champagne Urbana, DePaul University, and Wright College, and St Xavier University. She has featured at a variety of venues including Woman Made Gallery, I Love Hip-Hop Symposium, Palabra Pura through Chicago's Guild Complex, as guest poet at 16th Street Theater, Berwyn IL., and with Sage Morgan Hubbard's Mixed Mamas at Link Hall, Chicago , IL. She was a finalist in the 2011 Gwendolyn Brooks Open Mic contest. Her one woman show, Barrio Love Song, was a finalist in Teatro Vista's 2012 YO SOLO festival.

Silvia Goldman
Silvia Goldman, uruguaya, radicada en Estados Unidos desde hace once años, aunque nueva en el área de Chicago. Poemas y artículos académicos suyos han sido publicados en revistas literarias de Latinoamérica, Estados Unidos y Europa. En el 2008 publicó su primer libro de poemas titulado Cinco movimientos del llanto. Doctora en Estudios hispánicos por la Universidad de Brown. Actualmente se desempeña como profesora asistente en North Central College. Sus áreas de interés incluyen poesía hispanoamericana contemporánea, literatura testimonial y estudios de la memoria

Teresa Vázquez
Teresa Vazquez released "Audio Chapbook 001: A Woman Loving" in

2000. She appears in March Abrazo Press's Between the Heart and the Land/Entre el corazón y la tierra. She holds a Bachelor's in Creative Writing from Oberlin College, and an MFA from the School of the Art Institute of Chicago.

Valerie Martinez

Valerie Martínez is a poet, translator, teacher, playwright, librettist, and collaborative artist. Her award-winning books of poetry include Absence, Luminescent, World to World, A Flock of Scarlet Doves, Each and Her, And They Called It Horizon and This is How It Began. Her most recent book, Each and Her (winner of the 2012 Arizona Book Award), was nominated for the Pulitzer Prize, the National Book Critics Circle Award, the PEN Open Book Award, the William Carlos William Award, and the Ron Ridenhour Prize. Her work has been widely published in journals, magazines, anthologies and media outlets including The Best American Poetry, the Washington Post, and the Poetry Foundation's Poetry Everywhere series.

Xánath Caraza

Xánath Caraza is a traveler, educator, poet and short story writer. She was named number one of the 2013 Top Ten "New" Latino Authors to Watch (and Read) by LatinoStories.com. Originally from Xalapa,Veracruz, Mexico, she has lived in Vermont and Kansas City. She has an M.A. in Romance Languages. She lectures in Foreign Languages and Literatures at the University of Missouri-Kansas City. Her upcoming short story collection, Lo que trae la marea, What the Tide Brings (2013) is from Mouthfeel Press. Her full-length book of poetry Conjuro (2012) is from Mammoth Publications and her chapbook Corazón Pintado: Ekphrastic Poems (2012) is from TL Press. Caraza writes the US Latino Poets en español column, a collaboration between Letras Latinas (Notre Dame University) and Periódico de Poesía (UNAM, Mexico). She won the 2003 Ediciones Nuevo Espacio international short story contest in Spanish and was a 2008 finalist for the first international John Barry Award. Caraza is an advisory circle member of the Con Tinta literary organization and a former board member of the Latino Writers Collective in Kansas City. She has taught in Mexico, Brazil, China, Spain and the US. Caraza is currently working on a collection of ekphrastic poems with the artist Juan Chawuk. Her Day of the Dead Art work has been exhibited at the Nelson Atkins Museum of Art, Kansas City, MO.

Xánath Caraza es viajera, educadora, poeta y narradora. Fue nombrada la autora latina número uno de los diez mejores "nuevos" autores para ver (y leer) en 2013 por LatinoStories.com. Su poemario, Conjuro, ha recibido los siguientes premios y reconocimientos: poemario finalista en la categoría,

'Ficción: Multicultural' de 2013 International Book Awards; segundo lugar en la categoría, 'Mejor libro de poesía escrito en español en los Estados Unidos' y mención honorífica para la categoría, 'Mejor Primer libro en español, Mariposa Award ambos reconocimientos como parte de 2013 International Latino Book Awards. Caraza ganó el concurso Internacional de Cuento en español de Ediciones Nuevo Espacio en 2003 y fue finalista del primer concurso internacional de cuento John Barry Award. Originalmente de Xalapa, Veracruz, México ha vivido en Vermont y la ciudad de Kansas. Tiene una maestría en Lenguas romances. Enseña en el departamento de lenguas extranjeras y literatura de la Universidad de Missouri en la ciudad de Kansas (UMKC). Su próximo poemario, Sílabas de viento lo publicará Mammoth Publications. Es autora de la colección de cuento, Lo que trae la marea/ What the Tide Brings publicado por Mouthfeel Press, 2013. Su poemario, Conjuro (2012) fue publicado por Mammoth Publications y su plaquette, Corazón Pintado: Ekphrastic Poems (2012) fue publicado por TL Press. Caraza escribe para La Bloga (labloga.blogspot.com) y también escribe la columna US Latino Poets en español, una colaboración entre Letras Latinas de la Universidad de Notre Dame en los Estados Unidos y Periódico de poesía de la UNAM en México. Además tiene la sección de poesía y narrativa en la Revista Zona de Ocio en México. Caraza fue juez para el concurso de periodismo José Martí en 2013 y ha organizado el National Poetry Month en la página de Con Tinta por dos años consecutivos, 2012 y 2013. Caraza es un miembro del círculo de consejeros, Con Tinta, una organización literaria en los EE. UU. y fue parte de la mesa directiva del Latino Writers Collective de la ciudad de Kansas. Ha enseñado en México, Brasil, China, España y los Estados Unidos. Su arte ha sido mostrado en el museo de arte Nelson-Atkins en la ciudad de Kansas.

Xenia Ruiz

Xenia Ruiz, born and raised in Chicago's Humboldt Park neighborhood, is the author of a novel, Choose Me (2005, Hachette Book Group). In 2006, she self-published Boricua Morena: Memoirs of a Humboldt Park Girl. Also in 2006, she received a writing grant from the National Association of Latino Arts & Culture. She is a graduate of Northwestern University and Northeastern Illinois University. She is the first prize recipient of Northwestern University's 59th Annual Iota Sigma Epsilon Fiction Contest. In 2012, she completed a writing residency at Ragdale Foundation in Lake Forest, Illinois and while there, was awarded The Adrienne Reiner Hochstadt Award. She lives in Chicago with her family.

Yolanda Nieves

Yolanda Nieves, born and raised in Chicago's Humboldt Park

neighborhood, is an award winning poet, playwright, director, educator, actress, and founder of The Vida Bella Ensemble (2009.) She is the author of two highly acclaimed poetry books, Dove over Clouds and The Spoken Body (Plainview Press), and has been widely published in literary, academic, and independent presses. For her artistic work Yolanda has been featured on Vocalo, WGN TV News, NPR, and other public media forums.

Yolanda Nieves is the winner of the American Educational Research Associations Dissertation of the Year Award for Arts-Based Research 2010, The Brown Girls' Chronicles. This play has been nationally acclaimed and performed coast to coast. She is an Associate Professor at Wright College in Chicago.

Zulema Moret

Zulema Moret

Poeta argentina, reside en Michigan, USA. Es Profesora de Literatura Latinoamericana en Grand Valley State University, donde coordina el programa de Estudios Latinoamericanos. Escribe poesía, narrativa, literatura infantil y juvenil, y crítica cultural. Ha coordinado talleres de escritura en Barcelona entre 1986-2000.

Ha publicado Cazadora de sueños (poesía, 2003); Noche de rumba (cuentos, 2002), Un ángel al borde de un volcán ardiendo (2007, poemas, en inglés, francés y castellano); Lo gris (Poesía, 2012), Apenas épica (selección de poemas, 2012), Mujeres mirando al sur: Poetas sudamericanas en USA (2004). Su obra poética ha sido traducida al inglés, al italiano y al alemán. Ha leído sus poemas en festivals internacionales, nacionales..

ABOUT THE AUTHORS

From diverse cultural backgrounds and existential circumstances; from a vast river of ethnical and geographical paths come the poets and writers included in this Cantología.
The Guild Complex is a community-based literary organization presenting and supporting diverse, divergent and emerging voices through innovative programs including performances and readings.
Palabra Pura promotes literary expression in more than one tongue through a monthly bilingual poetry reading featuring Chicano and Latino artists.
With an aim to foster dialogue through literature in Chicago and beyond, each evening pairs a local poet with a visiting writer along with an open mic to engage the interaction of diverse voices, ideas, and aesthetics.

The contents of this book were not curated, chosen or edited; they are the work of their respective authors who own the copyright to such works.

Pandora lobo estepario Press

www.ingramcontent.com/pod-product-compliance
Lightning Source LLC
Chambersburg PA
CBHW061457170626
46811CB00004B/1555